# New Mexico

by Patricia K. Kummer,
the Capstone Press Geography Department

**Content Consultant:**
Pat Concannon
Social Studies Consultant
New Mexico Department of Education

CAPSTONE PRESS
MANKATO, MINNESOTA

# C A P S T O N E    P R E S S
818 North Willow Street • Mankato, MN 56001
http://www.capstone-press.com

*Library of Congress Cataloging-in-Publication Data*
Kummer, Patricia K.
    New Mexico/by Patricia K. Kummer (Capstone Press Geography Department).
      p. cm.--(One nation)
    Includes bibliographical references and index.
    Summary: An overview of the history, geography, people, and living conditions of the state of New Mexico.
    ISBN 1-56065-580-1
    1. New Mexico--Juvenile literature. [1. New Mexico.]
    I. Capstone Press. Geography Dept. II. Title. III. Series.
F796.3.K86  1998
978.9--dc21

                         97-9056
                            CIP

# Table of Contents

# Fast Facts about New Mexico

**State Flag**

**Location**: In the southwestern United States
**Size**: 121,598 square miles (316,155 square kilometers)

**Population**: 1,685,401 (1995 United States Census Bureau figures)
**Capital**: Santa Fe
**Date admitted to the Union**: January 6, 1912; the 47th state

**Roadrunner**

**Largest cities**: Albuquerque, Las Cruces, Santa Fe, Roswell, Farmington, Clovis, Hobbs, Alamogordo, Carlsbad, Gallup

**Yucca flower**

**Nickname**: The Land of Enchantment
**State bird**: Roadrunner
**State flower**: Yucca flower
**State tree**: Piñon (nut pine)
**State song**: "O, Fair New Mexico" by Elizabeth Garrett

**Piñon (nut pine)**

# *Chapter 1*
# New Mexico's Pueblos

New Mexico has 19 pueblos. Pueblos are villages that Native Americans built hundreds of years ago. Some Native Americans still live in them today.

Early Pueblo people lived in adobe homes. Adobe homes were built with clay and straw bricks that were dried in the sun. Today, New Mexico's Pueblo people still build their homes this way. Adobe bricks are popular with other people as well.

Most of the pueblos stand in the Rio Grande valley between Albuquerque and Taos. The

**Most of New Mexico's 19 pueblos stand between Albuquerque and Taos.**

**Many pueblos are known for the pottery made there.**

Acoma, Laguna, and Zuni pueblos are west of Albuquerque.

## Sky City

Acoma Pueblo sits high on a mesa. A mesa is a flat-topped hill with steep sides. This mesa rises more than 367 feet (110 meters) above the ground. That is why Acoma is called Sky City.

People have lived at Acoma for about 1,000 years. It is the nation's oldest continuously lived-in village. The pueblo's adobe church is more than 350 years old. It was built when Spain controlled New Mexico.

The Acoma people are known for making thin, white pottery. They decorate it with black and orange designs.

## Other Pueblos

Other pueblos are also known for their pottery. Potters at San Ildefonso Pueblo make shiny, black pottery. The Zia sun symbol appears on most Zia pottery. This symbol is also on New Mexico's flag.

Of all the pueblos, Zuni Pueblo has the largest population. The Zuni people make beautiful silver and turquoise jewelry.

## Land of Enchantment

New Mexicans call their state The Land of Enchantment. Native American, Spanish, and North American cultures make life different and interesting. A culture is the way of life for a group of people. A warm, dry winter climate makes living in New Mexico comfortable.

New Mexico draws millions of visitors each year. Some decide to stay. Santa Fe and Taos attract writers and artists. Many retired people move to Albuquerque and Las Cruces.

# Chapter 2
# The Land

New Mexico is in the southwestern United States. It is the nation's fifth largest state. Mexico borders New Mexico in the southwest. Texas lies to the south and east. Oklahoma touches New Mexico's northeast corner.

Northwestern New Mexico is part of the Four Corners. New Mexico, Colorado, Utah, and Arizona meet there. This is the nation's only spot where four states touch.

## The Great Plains
The Great Plains cover the eastern third of New Mexico. High, grassy lands roll across the

**New Mexico is called The Land of Enchantment.**

**The Rio Grande river runs through the Rocky Mountains.**

northern plains. The Canadian River flows east across the plains.

Red Bluff Reservoir is in far southern New Mexico. It was formed by a dam on the Pecos River. It is also New Mexico's lowest point at 2,817 feet (845 meters) above sea level.

## The Rocky Mountains

The southernmost part of the Rocky Mountains stands in New Mexico. The mountains rise up in the north central part of the state. The Rocky Mountains extend up into Alaska.

New Mexico's highest point is Wheeler Peak in the Rockies. It stands in the Sangre de Cristo Mountains. The peak rises 13,161 feet (3,948 meters) above sea level.

## Basin and Range Country

Mountain ranges also rise in southern New Mexico. The Guadalupe Mountains are in the southeast. The Mogollon Mountains stand in the southwest.

Desert basins lie between the mountains. A desert basin is dry, bowl-shaped land. The Tularosa Valley is one desert basin.

The Chihuahuan Desert covers most of southwestern New Mexico. The Gila River runs west through the desert. Prickly pear and cholla cactuses grow there. Poisonous scorpions and tarantulas live in this desert.

## The Colorado Plateau

The Colorado Plateau covers northwestern New Mexico. The San Juan and Chaco rivers flow across the plateau. Mesas rise above the plateau. Acoma Mesa and Enchanted Mesa are two of these mesas.

## The Rio Grande Valley

The Rio Grande river runs through the center of New Mexico. It starts in Colorado. It cuts through New Mexico's Rocky Mountains. Then the Rio Grande continues south through the Basin and Range Country.

The Rio Grande provides some water for the desert. Cotton, fruits, and vegetables grow there.

## The Continental Divide

The Continental Divide zigzags through New Mexico's western mountains. The Continental Divide is a region of high ground that divides the river system. Rivers east of the Continental Divide flow toward the Gulf of Mexico. Rivers west of the Continental Divide run into the Pacific Ocean.

## Climate

New Mexico has a dry, warm, and sunny climate. It does not receive much rain. New Mexico's

mountains receive the most rain and snow. Little rain or snow falls on its deserts.

Summer temperatures often rise above 90 degrees Fahrenheit (32 degrees Celsius). Many winter days see temperatures of 40 degrees Fahrenheit (four degrees Celsius). Nights in the mountains are colder year-round. ·

# Chapter 3

# The People

New Mexico is growing quickly. Las Cruces is one of the fastest-growing cities in the nation. Many retired people have moved there. In 1995, Rio Rancho was named the nation's fastest-growing small city. National companies have built offices and factories there.

## Hispanic Americans

New Mexico has the largest percentage of Hispanic Americans of any state. About 38 percent of New Mexicans are Hispanic. Hispanics speak Spanish or have Spanish-speaking backgrounds. Many of them are the families of

**New Mexico has the largest percentage of Hispanic Americans in the United States.**

**The famous rock formation called Shiprock is on the Navajo reservation in New Mexico.**

early Spanish pioneers. Others trace their families back to early Mexican settlers. Many of New Mexico's Hispanics still speak Spanish.

The cities of Española and Santa Fe hold Spanish festivals called fiestas each year. Hispanics display arts and crafts at the fiestas. They perform Spanish music and dances.

### White Americans

White Americans make up 76 percent of New Mexico's population. Many whites arrived in the late 1800s. They came from eastern and midwestern states. Many also came from nearby Texas.

In the 1940s and 1950s, more whites came. They built military bases and government laboratories. Some of these people stayed in New Mexico.

More recently, whites have moved to New Mexico to retire. Many live in Taos, Silver City, Ruidoso, and Albuquerque.

## Native Americans

The nation's second-largest percentage of Native Americans live in New Mexico. Native Americans make up almost 10 percent of the state's population. Only Alaska has a larger percentage of Native Americans.

The Navajo and Apache have lived in New Mexico since the 1500s. Today, many of them live on reservations. A reservation is land set aside for use by Native Americans.

Some reservations in northwestern New Mexico have rich oil, natural gas, and uranium deposits. Uranium is a type of metal that is used

to produce nuclear energy. Nuclear energy is a powerful kind of energy.

Many Native Americans also live in pueblos. A different Native American group lives in each of the 19 pueblos. Some of their families have lived in New Mexico for more than 1,000 years.

Today, many Pueblo people work in Santa Fe and Albuquerque. Some have jobs at Los Alamos National Laboratory.

## Other Ethnic Groups

About 2 percent of New Mexicans are African Americans. Some of New Mexico's first African Americans worked as cowboys. Today, most of them live in the state's cities.

Asian Americans make up nearly 1 percent of New Mexico's population. Many Chinese Americans are researchers at Los Alamos.

**The Zuni people dress up for the Inter-Tribal Indian Ceremonial held in Gallup each year.**

# Chapter 4

# New Mexico History

People have been living in New Mexico for thousands of years. Tools thought to be 55,000 years old were found near Orogrande in 1990.

About 2,000 years ago, Anasazi and Mogollon people built villages on top of cliffs. The Anasazi and Mogollon came from the Pueblo people. The Pueblo included the Zuni, Taos, and Sandia people. The Navajo and Apache settled on the land in the 1500s.

## Spanish Control and Pueblo Revolt

In 1539, Spanish soldiers came north from Mexico. They claimed the new land for Spain. They called it New Mexico.

**Mogollon people built villages on top of cliffs.**

About 60 years later, Spanish settlers arrived. They built ranches and farms. In 1610, Santa Fe became Spanish New Mexico's capital.

Roman Catholic missionaries also arrived. A missionary is a person sent to do religious or charitable work in a territory or foreign country. They built missions among the Pueblo people. Many Pueblo were forced to become Christians.

In 1680, the Pueblo banded together. They were tired of people trying to change them. They killed hundreds of Spaniards. The rest of the Spaniards fled to Mexico. The Spaniards returned and recaptured New Mexico in 1692.

## Mexican Control and Mexican War

In 1821, Mexico gained its independence from Spain. The Southwest came under Mexican control. This included New Mexico.

Mexico allowed U.S. settlers to enter New Mexico. A U.S. trader opened the Santa Fe Trail in 1821. It linked Independence, Missouri, with Santa Fe.

Many people in the United States wanted to control the Southwest. They started the Mexican War (1846-1848). In 1846, the U.S. Army captured Santa Fe.

**Missionaries built missions among the Pueblo people.**

The United States won the war. New Mexico became a U.S. territory. Thousands of U.S. settlers moved there.

### Indian Wars and Cattle Wars

Many settlers moved onto Apache and Navajo lands. Native Americans led raids against the settlers. U.S. troops fought the Native Americans.

In the 1860s, U.S. troops forced the Navajo and Apache to leave their homelands. They moved the Native Americans to a reservation on the Pecos River. In 1868, the Navajo returned to northwestern New Mexico.

The Apache fought U.S. control for 20 years. They were led by Apache leader Geronimo. He refused to let the Apache give up. In 1886, Geronimo finally surrendered.

Cattle ranchers and merchants fought for control of Lincoln County. This area is just southeast of the middle of the state. This fight was called the Lincoln County War (1876-1878).

One rancher hired William Bonney to help him. During the Lincoln County War, Bonney became known as the outlaw Billy the Kid. The Lincoln County sheriff killed Billy the Kid in 1881.

## Statehood

Railroads opened in New Mexico in the 1870s. They brought thousands of settlers.

Gold and silver mining grew quickly in southwestern New Mexico. Texas cattle ranchers moved into the southeastern part of the territory. By 1910, New Mexico had 327,301 people.

**Geronimo led the Apache in their fight to keep their land.**

In 1912, New Mexico became the 47th state. Santa Fe was named the state capital. It is the oldest capital city in the United States.

In the 1920s, people discovered oil in New Mexico. Oil fields flourished in the northwest and the southeast.

## World War II

The United States entered World War II (1939-1945) in 1941. Many Navajo fought in the Pacific. They made a code in the Navajo language. The code was used to send secret messages. The Japanese could not break the code.

In 1943, government scientists arrived at Los Alamos. They developed the atomic bomb. The atomic bomb is a powerful explosive. It destroys large areas and leaves behind dangerous elements. In July 1945, the government exploded the first atomic bomb. This happened in the desert near Alamogordo. In August, the United States dropped atomic bombs on Japan. Japan surrendered, and the war ended.

## Continued Growth

Since the war, New Mexico has been a research center and testing ground. At Los Alamos,

**The National Atomic Museum in Albuquerque shows people how the atomic bomb was first made in New Mexico.**

scientists study ways to use nuclear energy. Sandia National Laboratories in Albuquerque develops weapons and uses military inventions to help people when there is not a war. White Sands Missile Range tests weapons.

In the 1990s, trade with Mexico grew. A border crossing opened at Sunland Park in 1993. The North American Free Trade Agreement (NAFTA) started in 1994. That year, New Mexico's exports to Mexico increased by 33 percent.

# Chapter 5
# New Mexico Business

Service industries are New Mexico's biggest businesses. They include government work and tourism. Manufacturing, farming, and mining are also important in the state.

## Service Industries
Government work is New Mexico's leading service industry. Albuquerque and Los Alamos have government laboratories. Scientists there study how to use nuclear energy. New Mexico also has many military bases. Holloman Air Force Base is home to the Stealth fighter jet.

Tourism is another large service industry. About 7 million tourists visit New Mexico each

**Mining is an important New Mexico business.**

**Albuquerque is New Mexico's leading manufacturing area.**

year. They spend almost $3 billion. Hotels, restaurants, and ski resorts take in most of this money.

## Manufacturing and Mining

Albuquerque is New Mexico's leading manufacturing area. Many electronics companies have plants there. They make parts for computers, telephones, and military equipment.

New Mexico also has many oil refineries. The refineries are located close to the oil fields. Oil and natural gas are New Mexico's leading mineral products. They are mined in northwestern and southeastern New Mexico.

Coal and uranium are mined in northwestern New Mexico. Copper mining takes place in the southwest. New Mexico is a leading producer of molybdenum and potash. Molybdenum is used to strengthen steel. Potash is used for farm fertilizer.

## Agriculture

The state's leading farm product is beef cattle. Cattle graze on the Kiowa National Grasslands in northeastern New Mexico. Sheep graze in the southeast and the northwest.

New Mexico is a leading producer of chile peppers and pecans. They grow in the Rio Grande valley. Most of this cropland is irrigated. Irrigated means watered with a system of pipes, canals, or sprinklers. Grapes, apples, and cotton grow in the Rio Grande valley, too. Wheat, sorghum, and peanuts grow on the eastern plains. Most of this land is not irrigated.

# Chapter 6
# Seeing the Sights

New Mexico is an exciting place to visit. Some visitors explore volcanoes, caves, and dunes. Others visit pueblos, reservations, and cities. Some also ski, hunt, or fish.

## Northeastern New Mexico

Capulin Volcano National Monument stands in northeastern New Mexico. This volcano erupted about 10,000 years ago. Today, visitors can walk down into the center of the volcano. Early people probably saw Capulin erupt. Scientists who study old things found 10,000-year-old spearpoints near Folsom. These weapons are displayed at the Folsom Man Museum.

**White Sands National Monument is in southeastern New Mexico. It has the world's largest gypsum dunes.**

Santa Rosa is south of Capulin. It is famous
for the Blue Hole. This natural pool is 81 feet (24
meters) deep. Its blue water is crystal clear.
Divers in the pool can look up and see people
watching them.

## Southeastern New Mexico
Roswell is in southeastern New Mexico. Some
people believe alien spaceships crashed there.
Today, Roswell has the International UFO
Museum and Research Center.

Carlsbad Caverns National Park is south of
Roswell. It has one of the world's largest cave
systems. The caverns hold beautiful rock
formations. Some look like waterfalls.

Alamogordo is northwest of Carlsbad. Many
people visit its International Space Hall of Fame.
Space pioneers from 14 countries are honored
there. Space pioneers studied or explored space.

White Sands National Monument is just west
of Alamogordo. The world's largest gypsum
dunes rise 60 feet (18 meters) there. Gypsum is a
mineral used to make plaster. White Sands

Missile Range surrounds the dunes. In 1945, the first atomic bomb was tested there.

## Southwestern New Mexico

Las Cruces is southwest of the dunes. This is New Mexico's second-largest city. It is in the lower Rio Grande valley. Fields of chile peppers are nearby. New Mexico State University is in Las Cruces. Some students there study ways to grow new kinds of chile peppers.

Elephant Butte Reservoir is north of Las Cruces. This is New Mexico's largest lake made by humans. Fishers catch bass and catfish there. It is a popular place for swimming, too.

Gila National Forest is west of the reservoir. Gila Cliff Dwellings National Monument is in the forest. Ancient people lived there about 1,800 years ago. Visitors can hike to these cliff homes.

## Northwestern New Mexico

Gallup is in far western New Mexico. Pueblos and reservations surround this town. Acoma, Zuni, and Navajo people trade there.

Each year, Gallup hosts the Inter-Tribal Indian Ceremonial. Thousands of Native Americans attend. They perform dances and display pottery, jewelry, and blankets.

The Jicarilla Apache Reservation is northeast of Gallup. Visitors can hunt bear, deer, and elk there. People can fish for trout in the reservation's many lakes.

## North Central New Mexico

North central New Mexico has 16 of the state's 19 pueblos. Four well-known cities are also in this part of New Mexico. They are Taos, Los Alamos, Santa Fe, and Albuquerque.

Taos attracts artists and skiers. About 100 art galleries have paintings for sale. Sipapu is the state's oldest ski area.

Los Alamos is southwest of Taos. It is home to Los Alamos National Laboratory. In the 1940s, scientists developed the atomic bomb there.

Santa Fe is just southeast of Los Alamos. Santa Fe is New Mexico's capital. It has the nation's only round capitol building. It is shaped like a Zia sun symbol.

El Rancho de Las Golondrinas is south of
Santa Fe. This is a Spanish ranch from the 1700s.
Visitors can tour the ranch's 25 buildings and its
pepper fields.

Albuquerque is farther south. This is New
Mexico's largest city. It has many big companies
and new buildings. Spanish adobe buildings,
however, still stand in Albuquerque's Old Town.

# New Mexico Time Line

**53,000 B.C.**—People are living in New Mexico.

**A.D. 200-1300**—Anasazi and Mogollon people build cliff homes in northwestern New Mexico.

**A.D. 1150-1325**—Pueblo live along the Rio Grande.

**1500s**—The Apache and Navajo enter New Mexico.

**1539**—Spanish explorers come to New Mexico.

**1598**—Juan de Oñate establishes New Mexico's first permanent European colony.

**1610**—Santa Fe becomes the Spanish capital; work begins on the Palace of the Governors.

**1680**—Pueblo Indians rebel against Spanish rule and throw out the Spanish colonists.

**1692**—Diego de Vargas captures Santa Fe for Spain.

**1821**—Mexico gains its independence from Spain; New Mexico becomes part of Mexico; the Santa Fe Trail opens.

**1848**—Mexico gives New Mexico and other southwestern lands to the United States.

**1853**—New Mexico's land south of the Gila River becomes part of the United States.

**1862-1864**—Kit Carson defeats the Mescalero Apache and the Navajo.

**1876-1878**—Cattle ranchers and merchants battle one another for control of Lincoln County.

**1886**—The Apache War ends with the surrender of Geronimo.

**1912**—New Mexico becomes the 47th state.

**1916**—Mexican bandits raid Columbus, New Mexico, during the Mexican Revolution.

**1920s**—Oil is discovered in New Mexico.

**1930**—Carlsbad Caverns National Park opens.

**1945**—The first atomic bomb is tested near Alamogordo.

**1950**—Uranium is discovered in New Mexico.

**1970s**—The San Juan-Chama project brings water to north central New Mexico.

**1980**—The Very Large Array telescope is completed near Socorro.

**1991**—King Juan Carlos I of Spain visits Santa Fe.

**1992**—The Waste Isolation Pilot Plant near Carlsbad is approved for radioactive waste storage.

**1993**—A border crossing opens at Sunland Park, New Mexico, across from Juarez, Mexico.

**1994**—NAFTA goes into effect, increasing trade between Mexico and the United States.

**1995**—For $250 million, some Mescalero Apache agree to store nuclear waste on their reservation. The decision is not final.

**1996**—New Mexicans celebrate the 175th anniversary of the opening of the Santa Fe Trail.

# Famous New Mexicans

**Dennis Chavez** (1888-1962) Representative for New Mexico in the U.S. House (1931-1935) and Senate (1935-1962); born in Los Chavez.

**Ann Nolan Clark** (1896- ) Author of *Secret of the Andes* and other Native American stories; won Newbery Medal (1953); born in Las Vegas, N.M.

**Pete Domenici** (1932- ) U.S. Senator for New Mexico (1973-present); chair of budget committee (1981-1987 and 1995-present); born in Albuquerque.

**William Hanna** (1910- ) Creator of "Yogi Bear" and "The Flintstones" cartoons with partner Joseph Barbera; born in Melrose.

**Conrad Hilton** (1887-1979) Founder of worldwide chain of Hilton hotels; born in San Antonio, N.M.

**Georgia Lee Witt Lusk** (1893-1971) New Mexico's first woman representative in the U.S. House of Representatives (1947); born in Carlsbad.

**Bill Mauldin** (1921- ) Political cartoonist whose characters Willie and Joe became popular in the U.S. army newspaper *Stars and Stripes*; won a Pulitzer in 1945 and 1959; born in Mountain Park.

**Maria Montoya Martínez** (1887-1980) Artist known for her black-on-black pottery; encouraged other Native Americans to continue their traditional arts; born at San Ildefonso Pueblo.

**Demi Moore** (1962- ) Actress who starred in *Ghost* and *Now and Then*; born in Roswell.

**Popé** (1630?-1692)—Leader of the Pueblo Revolt (1680) that drove the Spanish from New Mexico for 12 years; from the San Juan Pueblo.

**Bill Richardson** (1947- ) Diplomat who served New Mexico in the U.S. House of Representatives (1983-1997); backed the passage of NAFTA; appointed U.S. ambassador to the United Nations by President Clinton (1996).

**Harrison Schmitt** (1935- ) Scientist, astronaut, and politician who explored the moon (1972) and served New Mexico in the U.S. Senate (1977-1983); born in Santa Rita.

**Al Unser** (1939- ) and **Bobby Unser** (1934- ) Race car drivers; Al won the Indy 500 four times; Bobby won it three times; born in Albuquerque.

**Pablita Velarde** (1918- ) Artist and author who wrote and illustrated *Old Father Story Teller*, an Indian legend book; born at Santa Clara Pueblo.

# Words to Know

**adobe**—a building material made of clay and straw bricks that are dried in the sun; also the name of buildings made with these bricks

**cavern**—a large chamber in a cave

**Continental Divide**—a region of high ground that divides the river system; rivers to the west flow into the Pacific Ocean and rivers to the east flow into the Gulf of Mexico

**desert basin**—dry, bowl-shaped land

**irrigate**—to water with a system of pipes, canals, or sprinklers

**North American Free Trade Agreement**—a treaty signed by Canada, the United States, and Mexico to increase trade among the three countries; known as NAFTA

**pueblo**—the Spanish word for village; also the people who lived there

**reservation**—land set aside for use by Native Americans

**UFO**—initials for an unidentified flying object; things seen flying in the sky that some believe are from outer space.

# To Learn More

**Early, Theresa S**. *New Mexico*. Hello USA. Minneapolis: Lerner Publications, 1993.

**Fradin, Judith Bloom and Dennis Brindell Fradin**. *New Mexico*. From Sea to Shining Sea. Chicago: Children's Press, 1993.

**Hoyt-Goldsmith, Diane**. *Pueblo Storyteller*. New York: Holiday House, 1991.

**Keegan, Marcia**. *Pueblo Boy: Growing Up in Two Worlds*. New York: Cobblehill Books, 1991.

**Lovett, Sarah**. *Unique New Mexico: A Guide to the State's Quirks, Charisma, and Character*. Santa Fe, N.M.: John Muir Publications, 1993.

**Peterson, David**. *Carlsbad Caverns National Park*. Chicago: Children's Press, 1994.

# Useful Addresses

**Acoma Pueblo**
P.O. Box 309
Acoma, NM 87034

**American International Rattlesnake Museum**
202 San Felipe NW
Albuquerque, NM 87104

**Carlsbad Caverns National Park**
3225 National Parks Highway
Carlsbad, NM 88220

**Gila National Forest**
3005 East Camino del Bosque
Silver City, NM 88061

**Palace of the Governors**
Palace Avenue, Santa Fe Plaza
Santa Fe, NM 87501

**Pecos National Historical Park**
P.O. Box 418
Pecos, NM 87552

# Internet Sites

**City.Net New Mexico**
http://city.net/countries/united_states/new_mexico

**Travel.org—New Mexico**
http://travel.org/newmexi.html

**State of New Mexico**
http://www.state.nm.us

**Pueblo Cultural Center**
http://hanksville.phast.umass.edu/defs/independent/
PCC/PCC.html

# Index